D1669353

To Frankfurter Institut für Erziehungshilfen und Familienbegleitung e.V. Ambulante Hilfen zur Erziehung Höchst, for their invaluable support and resources, especially Mrs Martina Seyffer (Educational Specialist), whose expertise and encouragement were pivotal in my journey as single father

To the Law Office Schkottke-Wegner Reinarz for their legal professional support, especially the family law specialist lawyer Mrs. Nina Schlottke-Wegner

Evan Trimmis

"Legal Ties, Family Bonds"

Intro

Initiating a custody case against the mother of my children was an incredibly difficult decision. It's a decision that should only be made when absolutely necessary, driven by the need to protect the children. I wouldn't have taken this step if it wasn't essential. As a father seeking custody in Germany, I knew I was at a disadvantage, but I was unaware of the full extent of the challenges I would face in the years to come.

Having experience in multiple legislations, I was familiar with the basic principles of custody cases. I understood the importance of expert evaluations and the involvement of specialized psychologists. What I didn't anticipate, however, was the involvement of additional individuals and institutions such as the youth welfare service and a seemingly unnecessary **court assistant**, both of whom provided opinions on the case.

While these individuals are legally qualified to offer their perspectives, they are not required to have a comprehensive understanding of general law. Consequently, the legal discussions in the courtroom were often limited to family law. This raises the question: what happens when other legal issues are involved?

Modern legal professionals tend to be highly specialized, often overlooking the interactions between various legal fields. My case suffered from this narrow focus. The court and other institutions, including the police, chose to ignore facts and actions that fell under criminal law in order to keep the case within the bounds of family law.

Under these circumstances, I was forced to limit my arguments to what family law permitted. Suing the children's mother for parental negligence was not my preference, but it was the only way to secure custody. The court disregarded other factors that led me to seek custody, such as **inability to exercise parental responsibilities**. Even when the mother engaged in a criminal act that exposed the children to potential violence, while the case was ongoing, the court failed to consider the criminal case official in its custody decision.

Furthermore, the police neglected to investigate the criminal case, deeming it unimportant due to the ongoing custody dispute. This highlights a phenomenon known as "judicial economy," which allows judges to bypass certain procedures or examinations in order to expedite a case, as long as it doesn't adversely affect the outcome or provide grounds for appeal. However, my case goes beyond mere judicial economy – it involves institutions that deliberately ignored criminal acts and unexecuted administrative procedures.

In the end, the legal complexities and challenges of my custody case underscore the need for a more holistic approach to addressing the diverse legal issues at play.

The Defendant

Mental state

The mother of the children, who is acting in the current case as the defendant, rationalized her entrance into Germany as a protective measure, asserting that individuals in Greece were trying to harm her. This led to suggest that she might be suffering from mental stress and should seek therapy - a sentiment officially acknowledged by the youth welfare office. Additionally, the youth welfare office requested a mental health certificate from a recognized institution as a prerequisite for regaining custody of her children, a requirement implemented independently and before the court's involvement. However, the mother adamantly refused to comply with this requirement.

Given these circumstances, the logical conclusion would seem to be that the mother is not currently capable of adequately caring for two children. Yet, there is a prevailing silence. The court, the police, and the women's organizations that initially supported the mother have all astonishingly retreated from the case without any statement before the final decision.

The crucial question remains unanswered: is the woman mentally ill, dangerous, or in danger herself? As for the possibility of her being mentally ill, I would like to share my perspective.

It is apparent that the mother has experienced extremely challenging circumstances that have impacted her mental state. Presently, she seems to have difficulty understanding her environment. Interpreting Western reality through an African lens may lead to misinterpretations. In my view, what she needs is education - to grasp the norms and values of Western culture, learn to see the life in Europe according to Western cultural perspectives, understand the differences, and cease interpreting Western realities solely based on her traumatic experiences in Africa.

This is precisely what's occurring now as she navigates the integration process, viewing it as a necessary step to ensure survival in her current environment.

As for potential criminal involvement, she is a scared victim who never felt trust and continues to refuse to disclose more information about the identities or the methods behind her illegal travels across Europe and the use of fraudulent documents.

Immigration concern

As soon as the youth welfare office decided to place the children in an institution and temporarily suspend the mother's custody rights for their protection, swift action was essential to prevent both parents from losing custody. Beyond the stable residency requirement, the need for sole custody was crucial. However, this didn't imply that the mother couldn't see or interact with her children.

The mother expressed a strong desire to permanently reside in Germany, in Europe, and not return to Africa. While I sympathize with the mother's concerns, I did not consider her desire to be inherently wrong. However, it is important to note that my primary concern is the well-being and best interests of the children.

In immigration matters, we cannot underestimate the privileges that parents gain if their child is born in Germany. It is understandable to consider having a child born in Europe as a means of gaining a stay permit. However, I strongly disagree with the notion of having children solely for the purpose of obtaining accepted benefits.

The mother consistently expresses her desire to stay in Germany during her interactions with authorities, the judge, the youth welfare office, and other institutions.

While this attitude should work in my favor, unfortunately, it did not.

The mother's primary goal was to obtain a residency permit in Germany, a desire that seemingly overshadowed her wish to be a mother. Despite her apprehension being evident in court and with relevant institutions, there was no inquiry into how she managed to travel to Germany, even though this was a journey between European countries, with our first daughter without travel documents

Defense strategy

The mother's assertion that I'm unfit and even dangerous to the children appears misguided unless she can propose a viable custody solution to the court. She rejected, indirect, my sole custody request, indeed, but failed to provide the court with an alternative resolution for the custody issue. This left the court to decide between awarding sole custody to me or maintaining the previous joint custody arrangement.

However, how could a court choose to uphold joint custody considering the mother's allegations that I was a poor husband, father, and potentially a criminal?

In the ongoing custody case, I have requested sole custody, while the opposing party has not presented any custody proposition thus far. Instead, they have chosen to oppose my request by attempting to portray me as unfit to assume custody responsibilities. This strategy is completely incomprehensible, considering that I am currently the only one capable of keeping the children out of a childcare institution.

An inexplicable strategy, especially considering that the defendant has consistently expressed, in court, during hearings, and in meetings related to this case, the importance of staying in Germany. She has emphasized her desire to remain where the children reside and have expressed the wish for the children to stay in Germany as well. Based on her verbal requests, which were never formally submitted in writing, up to this time, it is evident that her primary concern was not the well-being of the children but rather her own residency permit in Germany. To obtain a residence permit in Germany, she must be involved in childcare, even with restricted custody rights, provided the children are not under state guardianship. Why did she attempt to portray me as incapable of childcare without reclaiming back her suspended custody rights?

Bound by the constraints of time, I was keen to expedite the case to avoid any unnecessary prolongation. It was essential for me to utilize the full range of legal resources at my disposal to conclude the case swiftly and definitively in the first instance.

Furthermore, the mother, who had lived in Germany for the last five years under a temporary deportation reprieve, was able to extend her stay every few months by showcasing her role in childcare. Despite expressing fear of deportation, she contradicted herself by providing falsified evidence to portray me as an unfit father, even involving the police in her allegations, leaving a significant impact on the case.

The defendant's attorney described her approach to the court in her opening statement, vigorously contesting every aspect of the case. Her outrage was so intense that she even filed criminal charges against me in a civil case without asking for the case to be suspended. The defendant's plan also included protesting the youth welfare office's decision to take the kids into custody. She did so despite the fact that the one-month window for submitting such objections had already passed.

This approach was not arbitrary. A central aspect of the defendant's strategy was to paint herself as a victim, seemingly manipulating everyone. Something that the defendant lawyer partly achieved. The primary attempt by the other party to level criminal charges against me seemed to be based on mere speculation. Accusing me of criminal behavior for a time I lived out of Germany could tarnish my reputation in the eyes of the court.

Additionally, these accusations might not be investigated due to jurisdictional conflicts, as crimes are typically investigated by authorities in the location where they occurred. However, it raises a question: why would the defendant choose, later, to file a denunciation against me with German authorities, thus tailoring the accusations to fit local legal competences? This action exposes the defendant to the risk of being charged with false denunciation. Under German law, this could potentially lead to a criminal trial against the defendant's client

In a speculative and ironic twist, the defendant's response to the case includes an attempt to shift her obligations regarding the children's citizenship status onto me. This likely represents the defendant's legal representative's tactic to shirk responsibilities or, quite possibly, it's a consequence of inadequate case investigation from her legal representation – a common trait in contemporary civil law practice!

While she spent most of her response accusing me and questioning my criminal state, she failed to clearly express her position on my request for sole custody. Additionally, she neglected to provide any proposal for resolving the children's custody issue. As a result, there is a lack of explanation regarding how she plans to contribute to the upbringing of the children.

I could possibly accept such an amateurish response if the defendant were acting alone. However, she has legal representation, the support of one or more women's organizations, and a self-proclaimed witness. While not all of them need to possess legal education to appear in court or provide their opinions, it is expected that her lawyer will have a solid understanding of the law.

Part of the Defendant attorney strategy was also recruiting a falls witness. Which would witness seeing me to use violence against the children or listening to me to talk shameful to the kids! And indeed, the defendant lawyer considered the witness as her best asset in this case, expressing in the court in every chance that she got a witness! After counting all this time her first lawyer advertised her witness, it's kind of strange that the witness finally never occurred and never got heard during the process

The Court and the Law

The hearing

Taking in consideration that up to the moment I decided to file petition to the court requesting sole custody my knowledge about the German legal system was extreme limit, but I had a general knowledge of the Family law in other jurisdictions.

The German family court system, or "Familiengericht", is a specialized jurisdiction within the German legal system that handles family matters.

In my experience I worked before with family law cases in roman law-based systems where Family law is a part of the Civil law or systems where Family law is code on its own.

Initiation of Proceedings: Family court proceedings typically commence when my petition for sole custody was filed.

Role of the Judge: The family court judge plays an active role in the proceedings. Unlike in some adversarial systems, the German system is inquisitorial. This means that the judge takes on a more investigative role, guiding the proceedings, asking questions, and ensuring that all necessary facts are revealed.

Examination and Cross-examination: Parties and witnesses give statements before the court. The process is less confrontational than in systems I experienced up to this time. After each party has given their account, the judge asked questions for clarification or to challenge the statement. The judge's examination was extremely limited, without leading questions and mostly very limited around family law matters only. Taking into consideration the defendant's arguments and potential evidence, I accepted a more aggressive examination of both parties, but it never happened.

The lawyers up to this time, except preparing the paperwork and submitting the arguments in written form, determined the strategy of course, intervenes in any moment protecting the rights of their clients.

Role of Third Parties

Youth Welfare Office: was an active part of the case, in my eyes the youth welfare office played a role as the procurator plays in other jurisdictions after the procurator submits the petition. They offer opinions, oversees visitations, and in my case, they take temporary custody of children suspending the mother's custody rights and gave me limited sole custody, waiting a court decision to clarify the issue. Generally, in the German Family court system, the Youth Welfare Office's reports and recommendations are heavily considered by the court.

Custody Evaluators and Psychologists: In disputed custody cases, the court might order a psychological evaluation of the parents and children to determine what custody arrangement would be in the child's best interests.

Family court assistance: This is an independent person appointed by the court to represent the child's interests. They ensure that the child's voice and needs are represented in the proceedings.

The court seemed to try to give a decision that will make everyone happy! And this is not exactly something that happens in vain. Generally, the German family court system, and as general about Family law, is encouraged parties to find amicable solutions instead of digging into arguments or evident, the court tried to keep it as simple as possible even if the defendant's arguments were extreme furious.

Judge Responsibility

In Germany, the court system operates under civil law tradition, which differs greatly from the adversarial system. Judges, including those in family courts, play a more active role in court proceedings, including the questioning of witnesses. This system places the judge at the forefront of establishing the facts of the case, rather than the attorneys conducting the examinations.

This was evident during my own custody case. The judge led the questioning, sought clarifications as needed, and left little room for attorneys to direct queries. What struck me most was the absence of leading questions. The judge is tasked with pinpointing the key details to reach a conclusion.

Under this system, it is the judge's responsibility to identify any missteps or lack of legal logic in the case. This was pertinent in my situation, where the mother's defensive strategy was to portray me as unfit for custody. This choice risked leaving our children without parental care and potentially placed them in an institution.

Certainly, one could interpret the mother's strategy as a selfless act aimed at protecting her children. However, the court never made efforts to investigate the true motive behind the created legal gap. The German legal system does not grant anyone, except the judge, the authority to examine this aspect, further complicating the situation.

During the proceedings, the judge was changed without providing any explanation to the parties involved. Initially, I was unsettled by the change as I had more confidence in the first judge, considering her background in the prosecutor's office before specializing in family law. However, the new judge show signs of populism, which made me, reconsider the impact of the change.

After the apprehensive mother articulated her fears regarding possible deportation, the judge responded with the most populistic reassurance I had ever witnessed in a court hearing. She declared, "As a judge, I assure you, no one will deport you from Germany based on the length of your children's residence here. If anyone says otherwise, report directly to me!"

This response stunned me. I found myself in the midst of the most populist court hearing I had ever attended yet felt helpless to change anything. To my surprise, no one else seemed to share my dismay, not even the present lawyers!

It seems germane to question the transparency of a system where false allegations and perjury seemingly have no bearing on the proceedings. The critical role of the judge in such a system becomes clear - their duty is not only to gather facts but also to ensure justice is served.

What I was awaiting from the judge was to address directly and officially to the defendant that such an answer to the submitted petition of the plaintiff is off topic and unacceptable in the scope of this court process. These are serious allegations, and the defendant should consider presenting the criminal case to a prosecutor, up to this time the court can't accept such an answer. Here are significant parts missing in the defendant's answer. First there is totally missing to take a state about how does the defendant plan to contribute to the upbringing of the children, and of course what exactly is the defendant's opinion about how should solve the custody issue. Of course, there are more mistakes in the defendant's statement but this I was awaiting from the judge to officially add to the record of this court case.

Legal Representation

The primary responsibility for establishing the strategy in a case and guiding a defendant towards a different approach typically rests with their legal counsel. Lawyers are trained to understand the law and to advise their clients on the most effective way to navigate their specific legal circumstances. It's crucial for the **litigants** to have competent legal representation to ensure their rights are protected and their case is presented as strongly as possible.

Ultimately, the responsibility to identify the incorrect strategy and guide the defendant towards a different approach in the case falls upon the defendant's legal counsel. It is their duty to provide informed, strategic advice and to ensure their client's best interests are served throughout the legal proceedings.

When I recognized the flawed legal situation, I realized my potential actions were more constrained than anyone else's in the courtroom. Something that my attorney successfully pointed up and complained verbally during the first hearing. However, this legal gap wasn't my sole concern regarding the case.

I consulted with other lawyers as well, about the criminal allegation, or about seeking advice on the case's constitutionality. At best, the law firms I approached provided a refusal. However, most of the firms I contacted did not respond to my inquiries at all!

As I mentioned, the mother recruited a falls witness. Which would witness seeing me to use violence against the children or listening to me to talk shameful to the kids! And indeed, the defendant lawyer considered the witness as her best asset in this case, expressing in the court in every chance that she got a witness! After counting all this time her first lawyer advertised her witness, it's kind of strange that the witness finally never occurred and never got heard during the process. And here are a few theories, why would the witness never express her opinion to the case. First the witness is a social worker who used to help different minorities in the integration process. She met the defendant a few months before this case started. Even if the defend lawyer considered the witness as an asset, it's easy to object to such a witness, and as soon as she is a social worker on her own, that would properly put her job in jeopardy. Committing perjury is a crime, even in Germany! But there was another procedural problem. The court assistant, in a totally amateur way, said openly in the court that she knew the witness and except this, the witness made the translator during her obligatory meeting with the defendant prior to the court hearing! Really, how more amateurish could that be? A violation of the court procedural rules, expressed openly without excitement in front of the court, who exactly could do that?

Finally, I'm really wondering how a lawyer could suggest to her client to include the police, taking into consideration she wasn't "clean" on her own. First, I consider the lawyer was in a delusion believing blindly what the defendant told her without exanimating the penal allegations, despite the lawyer's general knowledge about the law the missing practice of penal cases could be fatal.

The Expert

Considering the German court system, with its empowered judges and the restrictive rights afforded to lawyers during hearings, it's critical to highlight the legal gap in the current case. This gap, born out of the mother's strategic maneuvering, could only be identified by the two lawyers and the judge. The other attendees weren't expected to comprehend the complexities of the legal chasm formed. Nevertheless, this legal gap ultimately strengthened the viewpoint for raising the children in a care facility, rather than with their parents.

As previously mentioned, the court sought the opinion of an expert tasked with assessing the parental fitness of both parties. This required a comprehensive evaluation of all relevant factors and the preparation of a written report.

However, the questions posed to the expert by the court were highly specific and professional in nature. Given that the expert is an experienced family psychologist with deep knowledge of child behavior and parental issues, this is understandable.

During my interrogation, the expert requested documents proving my innocence against the criminal allegations made by the children's mother, as well as evidence supporting my claims about the mother's behavior. Having previously been denied the opportunity to present my proof or narrative to the police or court, I saw this as my chance to voice my side and submit extra supporting documentation. However, this was not the evidence the expert was seeking, a point that was negatively reflected, later, in the written report.

Despite the expert's extensive experience in custody hearings and role as a court expert, there was a notable lack of legal knowledge. This is evident in the fact that the expert asked me to prove my innocence before initiating their investigation, instead of asking the court to do so.

Professionals in psychology, childcare, and parenting often focus on specific theoretical problems, rarely if ever grappling with real-life issues. A psychologist in Germany could pen countless pages on the psychological reasons behind a simple choice yet fail to address practical problems such as a furious outburst.

This is exactly what happened at one of my daughter's expert meetings. She stopped cooperating, began screaming, and started to throw and destroy things around her. The expert promptly called me to pick her up. Upon arriving just minutes later, I found my daughter, having escaped the institution, was barefoot and outside of the institution, on the street, with social workers and psychologists unsuccessfully attempting to calm her down. She finally felt safe upon seeing me, hugging me, and asking me to take her home. This wasn't an isolated incident; there were other similar occasions where I had to pick up my daughter early from the expert meeting because they couldn't manage the situation.

While in every passionate outburst of the child, my intervention consistently proved both crucial and triumphant. However, curiously, it never found mention within the extensive final expertise.

One question I'd like to pose is about the financial cost to the German government for this 250-pages expert report from the psychologist. How much did this expert psychologist earn for offering an opinion on a legal case without having any comprehensive understanding of the law?

The manner in which the expert testimony was given and handled was, in itself, a gross miscarriage of justice. Given the significant weight that a judge typically places on expert opinions, it is frustrating that so much time was invested into procuring one, only for the court to largely disregard it in its final decision.

The court provided limited clarity on my alternatives, the potential pool of experts they could select for opinion, or the basis for their choice of a specific expert. I was never consulted, and my understanding of the process was minimal.

To clarify, I had the right at any point to request a change of expert or to challenge the validity of the expert testimony through a different institution. However, considering my time constraints, I was hesitant to take such a risk.

Moreover, the process was extremely taxing for the children. After all, all actions should be in the children's best interest, shouldn't it?

Following the initial hearing, the court designated a specific private institute to draft the expert's testimony. This same institute was tasked with overseeing meetings between the mother and children and facilitating parental consultation sessions. Surely, locating these various functions within one entity simplified matters for the court compared to sourcing three separate establishments or individuals for the tasks.

I was curious about whether the three distinct functions involved in my case were interconnected. This arose from my personal interactions with the psychologist overseeing the meetings between the mother and children, and facilitating parental consultation sessions. This is the same psychologist who as well as the main psychologist on several occasions requested that I pick up my daughters early from their sessions due to difficulties in managing the situation, necessitating my intervention to maintain control.

Consequently, I requested the court to obtain an additional written report from the lead psychologist who oversees these functions. However, I anticipated that this report would likely align with the initial psychological assessment. Challenging the main expert's opinion could reveal that these processes – the family consulting sessions, the supervised mother-child meetings, and the preparation of the main expert report – are not interrelated and operate independently. On the other hand, such a revelation could potentially harm the institution's reputation and the credibility of their report to the court. It might also jeopardize the employment of the secondary psychologists and expose potential pressure they face in expressing their independent opinions.

The report from the secondary psychologist seemed to support the primary psychological report, omitting details about incidents or issues discussed during their sessions with the parties involved. Despite my request, the court did not summon this secondary psychologist to testify as a witness. Furthermore, although some sessions involving me and all the supervised meetings between the children and their mother were audio or video recorded, this evidence was not presented in court, despite my requests.

This situation suggests that all functions within this institution are interconnected, with each one contributing to the main expert's assessment in a manner deemed confidential. This raises concerns about the impartiality of the institution and could potentially affect the integrity of the court proceedings. Perhaps this is why the court didn't hesitate to approve my suggestion, after the expert's report submitting, to assign the supervised meetings and parental consulting sessions to different institutions and to implement these changes immediately, potentially establishing a new entity for supervised meetings or family consulting sessions.

Nevertheless, I question whether bias played a part in the court's initial decisions or if this is standard practice for family cases in Germany. Neither myself nor my lawyer, nor even the youth welfare office (which has supported my attempt to gain sole custody) raised any objections. It leads me to wonder whether any of the parties noticed any bias in the court's selection of this specific institute.

In Germany, there are certain untouchable entities - people, organizations, or businesses deeply embedded in German culture. Criticizing them is not recommended. Therefore, publicly expressing an opinion on the chosen institute is not a step everyone in Germany is willing to take. When I, finally, voiced my concerns, I was met with indifference.

Challenging the decision of the institute, which was court-appointed, would fundamentally question long-standing practices. If this case were to reach the highest courts, a motion against the chosen institute might have to be pursued outside German courthouses.

The Institute's environment proved to be very hostile. I can't help but wonder if the court's decision to rely on a specific institute signifies bias, or even discrimination. Specifically, the institute, which is almost entirely run by women, was asked to evaluate a man's request for sole custody. This choice left me questioning the court's impartiality.

The psychologist rendered judgments about me based on my life narrative, but I was never given an opportunity to clarify or dispute these interpretations. Some facts, which I considered assets, were interpreted as signs of sociopathy or considered unacceptable. These were aspects of my life I believed would enrich my children's upbringing process, but in fact, I was never asked for an explanation by either the psychologist or the court.

Presenting my case in court could clarify matters that remained vague throughout the process. For instance, my experience of living in different countries during my 20s and early 30s was misconstrued by the psychologist as a symptom of sociopathy. However, my international lifestyle broadened my perspective on various cultural nuances, traditional influences on peoples' lives globally, and the scope of legal systems.

In my view, law is a dynamic entity tailored by lawmakers to fit the society it serves. Each society thus has laws that reflect its unique needs. If given a chance to explain in court, I would have clarified that my international relocation was driven by my career ambitions and the desire to gain firsthand knowledge of diverse legal and law systems. In part, I have accomplished this.

Moreover, the psychologist critiqued the methods by which I was raised during the 80s. Considering that the psychologist, who was over 60 years old at the time the expert opinion was formulated, experienced the 80s first-hand, she would understand the significant shifts in child-rearing practices since then. Given that I spent part of my childhood in Germany, her objections to my upbringing during my time outside of Germany seem discriminatory. This, in and of itself, casts a shadow of bias over the expert opinion.

Injunctive but not restrictive, the expertise criticized badly the fact that no birthday party in our house was held without explaining that my daughter's birthday was during the limitations due to the Corona pandemic! So we decided only to make a party in the daycare institution where my daughter use to attend after school, as nobody had the courage to challenge this fact direct to the expert questioning, if I simple where questioned about why did I choose don't to have an extended birthday party with more invited people I could just answer that what the expert didn't mention that we were in the middle of lock down restrictions that time.

Conclusions

My Strategy

My primary reason for seeking sole custody of our children from the court was not solely related to the mother's incident of violence against our children causing the involvement of the youth welfare office, forcing the kids in a children protection facility for a period of about 5 weeks. While I unequivocally condemn any form of violence against children, it was not the decisive factor that led me to question the mother's capabilities. I was chiefly concerned with her mindset of using the children primarily to secure a favorable immigration status. My fear is that once she attains this status, she may neglect her parental responsibilities. I have voiced this concern in some non-judicial interactions, despite facing considerable criticism.

Contrary to my personal beliefs, presenting evidence to substantiate these concerns in court shouldn't be challenging, provided I am given the opportunity to do so.

Another perplexing issue is how the mother managed to travel from Greece to Germany with our first daughter without proper documents, using a false identity. This is especially alarming considering the stringent requirements for custodial permission when minors travel across the Greek borders, even within the

Schengen area, as stipulated by European Union regulations (DIRECTIVE 2004/38/EC OF THE EUROPEAN PARLIAMENT AND OF THE COUNCIL). Regardless of jurisdictional constraints, this act questions her decision-making as a parent.

Moreover, her criminal conduct in Germany, resulting in her arrest on two occasions - the latter occurring during ongoing court proceedings - happened in the presence of our children. This led the youth welfare office to propose court-ordered psychological therapy for the children.

My approach would not be to dwell on the arrests or the circumstances leading to them. While I couldn't ask the family court to examine direct these actions, I intend to highlight them as factual context, aiming to understand her state of mind during these incidents and her assessment of our children's welfare at the time of these episodes. Finally, for the first arrest, following the completion of the police investigation, there was no risk of self-incrimination[1], at this time, as soon as that case was already closed.

The most straightforward method to uncover this was to question the defendant directly. Even a direct examination from her attorney, or the judge, could reveal her mental state. Further, her responses regarding

---

[1] In Germany, like in many other legal systems, the principle of "nemo tenetur se ipsum accusare," translating to "no one is bound to accuse themselves," is upheld. This mandates that courts are obligated to inform individuals of their right to remain silent and the risks of self-incrimination.

her considerations for the children during her actions would have been illuminating. However, it seems no one in the German court is prepared to initiate these inquiries. Reflecting on these events, it appears I gained custody more due to fortunate circumstances. I'm uncertain if the outcome would have been the same had the defendant not explicitly exchanged her custodial rights over the children to maintain her residency in Germany.

Nonetheless, these are intricately complex strategies for a family court in Germany. Therefore, my attorney, who is highly skilled in family law, opted for a straightforward approach. She based her strategy on the recommendations of the youth welfare office and the violent incident, and the mother's capability to fill up her parental responsibilities, simply requesting custody in terms that the German court would comprehend and accept.

The disappointment

Every jurisdiction establishes its legal system based on its unique characteristics. When legislators draft or develop laws, they consider not only their personal views of justice but also the well-being and prosperity of society as a whole. On the other hand, Germany has a specific legal framework in place to promote the happiness of its citizens. I am not criticizing the way Germans organize their legal structures; rather, I feel trapped in a legal system that does not represent me.

In other legal systems, working in the law industry means accustomed to conducting extensive investigations for any case. Searching through statutes for evidence, create profiles of everyone involved in the proceedings, including the parties, judge, experts, and potential witnesses. However, in Germany, the system relies heavily on theoretical facts, codes, and laws.

In my own case, there was little need for investigation as I had compiled a substantial folder containing all the evidence necessary to support my claims. If criminal acts were involved, I was fully prepared to present them, and in civil or family cases, I had prepared for thorough cross-examination. However, I found myself in the wrong jurisdiction. The only part of my strategy that aligned with my lawyer's approach, who did an excellent job, was the psychological profiling of individuals, including myself. This is precisely where the defendant's first lawyer failed to understand her own client and allowed for a legal loophole, assuming she even recognized its existence.

I eagerly awaited the questioning process, which, to my disappointment, never came. The examination was conducted solely by the judge. While this should have marked the end of my prosecution plan, it did not.

Although I or my party could not lead the examination, the judge took charge. I was initially pleased to learn that the judge had previously practiced law in a prosecutor's office. However, the judge was unexpectedly replaced by a family law expert, ensuring that the case would be confined within the boundaries of family law without anyone taking notice. Nonetheless, the case reached a point where both judges should have recognized the legal loophole we were in and conducted investigations in that direction. As the judge was following the civil law tradition, having the highest authority and sole responsibility in the hearing, it was crucial for them to examine the parties thoroughly and ensure the defendant understood the strategy being applied.

Regrettably, the judge failed to examine the reasoning behind the defendant's chosen strategy and neglected to address the criminal allegations. They also failed to inquire if the parties understood the criminal allegations and the implications of a criminal investigation leading, eventually, to a suspension of the civil case. Even though the defendant's immigration concerns dominated the final result, no examination or question aimed at elucidating the matter was posed to the parties, despite the fact that both parties brought up the immigration concerns on multiple occasions during the hearing. The final decision openly affected the defendant's immigration status; under these circumstances, shouldn't the court seek the opinion of the immigration office by subpoenaing it under Joinder of third parties' procedure[2]?

What about the perjury, of course, if the defendant statements could classified as perjury under the actual circumstances?[3] What happened after the defendant

---

[2] In German civil law, the term "Joinder of third parties" (known as "Streitverkündung" in German) refers to a procedural mechanism whereby a party involved in a legal dispute can formally involve a third party in the ongoing litigation. This is typically done when the original party believes that the third party may be liable to them for all or part of the claim made against the original party or may have a related interest in the subject matter of the dispute.

When a joinder is made, the third party is notified of the litigation and can choose to participate in the proceedings. Depending on the specifics of the case and the extent of the third party's involvement, they may take an active role in the defense or merely observe the proceedings to protect their interests. The involvement of third parties in this manner ensures that all related issues and parties are adequately represented and that the final judgment takes into account the full spectrum of interests and liabilities.

[3] Section 153 of the German Criminal Code: This section stipulates that anyone who deliberately provides false testimony under oath before a court or a competent authority that has the power to administer oaths is liable to be convicted of perjury. This is akin to the concept of perjury in common law jurisdictions, where lying under oath during a legal proceeding is a criminal act.

The question is are the defendant's statements being

falsely accused me of criminal acts that I never committed? What about my criminal allegations against the defendant? The involvement of the police, who had barely questioned me as key witnesses, also needs to be

---

given under oath, taking in consideration that in German family court proceedings, as in other legal proceedings, the principle that governs testimonies and statements is grounded in the legal framework provided by the German Civil Procedure Code (Zivilprozessordnung, ZPO) and the German Criminal Code (Strafgesetzbuch, StGB). Whether statements made in a family court are considered to be under oath depends on the specific circumstances and the requirements of the court at the time the statements are made.

Family court proceedings are often more focused on finding solutions that are in the best interests of the family, particularly children, rather than strictly adhering to adversarial principles. As such, the use of sworn testimony is carefully considered and applied when absolutely necessary to ascertain the truth in matters critical to the court's decision-making process.

It's important for parties involved in family court proceedings to understand when their statements are being made under oath and the legal obligations and potential consequences that accompany sworn testimony. Legal advice from a qualified attorney can provide guidance on these matters, ensuring that individuals are fully informed about their rights and responsibilities when making statements in court.

addressed. What about my allegations that the mother's criminal behavior was intentional and premeditated, potentially involving third parties? I possess evidence supporting all these allegations, yet nobody wanted to examine them despite my written requests to the police. What about the contradictions in the defendant's deposition?

Regardless of the reasons behind the authorities' lack of action, whether it be due to my limited German proficiency, my fervent allegations, or the ongoing custody case, the fact remains that numerous pages of accusations, supported by substantial evidence against the defendant and further people, have gone unexamined.

I never tried to influence the mother to make a less favorable choice, nor did I ever beg or suggest that she cease seeing the kids. My issue stems from the fact that the mother moved about Europe for almost eight years under a false identity, crossed borders, and did other things that required outside assistance to be accomplished. I was aiming at those people, but I have no idea who they are. Consequently, neither the authorities nor I will ever know who they are, and they will be free to carry out their illegal acts without any issues.

Germany allowed a loop in her system by allowing all the people to come in during the refugee crises of 2015, and for that the world is thankful, indeed, but Germany never thought about regulating the law in that way all this made exceptions to find a solution!

I even try to solve my daughters' citizenship problem in Germany after getting custody, but the answer of the authorities was, solve the identity problem before directing to us!

The decision

The court decision that gave me sole custody of my children, under conditions, came with a short rezoning paragraph which wrote the following sentence:

"Both parties, as well as the Court assistant and the Youth Welfare Office, agreed that the children's primary residence should remain with the father. During the oral proceedings, the father assured that he would keep the children in Frankfurt and not move them to Greece or another neighboring country. The parents involved have agreed to transfer the health care authority, the right to handle school-related matters, and the right to make applications to authorities and agencies to the father, while continuing to share the right to determine the place of residence."

In this way, I indeed got custody of the children, but also got an indirect restricted order to stay in Germany exactly in Frankfurt. By granting joint authority over the children's residence, the court safeguards the mother's immigration status and implicitly endorses her use of the children to secure residency rights. This is achieved by granting her the authority to decide where the children will live, with the stipulation that their residence must be in Frankfurt, Germany, which also secures the mother's permit to stay. While the parents are mandated by the court's decision to maintain the children's residence in Germany, the same court has stripped the mother of all custodial rights except for determining where the children will reside. In this manner, the mother openly exchanges most of her custodial rights for her immigration status with the court's tacit approval. This court decision is not just a miscarriage of justice but is at least offensive for the mother and of course for the children too, who will come one day to interpret and understand this decision.

My primary goal was to move out of Germany before my children began schooling. This was not merely a statement I presented in court; I also embraced the consequences of this decision by willingly forgoing certain support from the welfare office, which becomes unavailable once I openly planned to leave Germany. However, due to the prolonged nature of the court proceedings, I had to alter my plans as both children commenced school before the court reached its final verdict.

The legal issue with this decision lies in the court's indirect determination of the children's residency, a concern officially raised after the defendant changed her legal representation. The principal criticism is that the residency order's basis wasn't the children's welfare. The plea to the court didn't demonstrate how residency in Germany, particularly Frankfurt, would benefit the children. Rather, the request overtly sought to secure residency in Germany and even solicited additional advantages to enable the mother to remain in Germany and exercise her limited custodial right to decide the children's residence.

This aspect of the proceedings is as intricate as the entire case. The judge had to step in at this point and dismiss the plea for extra benefits, which the defendant audaciously sought, deeming it a tactical error by the defendant's legal counsel. However, this was a calculated and fully conscious strategy executed by the defendant's second lawyer with utmost professionalism, aiming to extract as much as possible from the court by continually making new demands until the judge began to refuse.

Requests for specific government benefits, such as a free home or predetermined financial allowances, should be considered as a factor in granting custodial rights to the defendant. If these benefits are not granted, the defendant would be content with a guarantee of her continued residency in Germany.

At this point, the court had not only started to examine direct self-generated requests and evaluate them within the context it had created, but it also stepped out of the scope of the process, which should have primarily focused on the children's welfare—a point barely touched upon at this stage. To be clear, this overreach didn't persist for long; the judge intervened before matters could escalate. However, for a brief period, the manipulative tactics seemed to be effective.

Focusing on that way the whole custody battle around the immigration status of the mother instead of the welfare of the kids, and requests from the youth welfare office for special subversion psychological support of the children, or the long psychological report who asked special psychological treatment of the children and their parents were just ignored from the court. Nothing about the future of the under-supervision visitation rights of the children from their mother, finally there wasn't any request in that way from the site of the mother. Self the judge didn't ask, the court assistant worried openly about the immigration status of the mother instead of the welfare of the children and the welfare office, which was also present up to the end, took ex officio all those rights about deciding the visitations or support of the children exactly as would happen if the court never started.

Appealing this decision nobody seemed to want to do so. The mother didn't see anything offensive in that decision, the youth welfare office supported the residency of the children at the father, the procedural assistant concern was the immigration status of the mother which was guaranteed through this decision and me my concern is that my children, up to this time, remind without citizenship and whatever decision gives me the right to request citizenship at this moment was welcome.

I am profoundly unsettled by the court verdict. While the decision nominally grants me sole custody, it imposes an undue residency restriction. This constraint, paradoxically, seems more tailored to securing the mother's immigration status rather than addressing the children's welfare, an approach I find to be a flagrant miscarriage of justice.

The virtue of justice

The law has both theoretical and practical facets. The German legal system effectively narrows the gap between these two, resulting in a rigid legal framework with almost no exceptions. This leaves little room for interpretation or incentives but creates potential for biases.

It's noteworthy that the first opposing lawyer's response to my sole custody request deviated from standard tactics. I suspect third-party intervention, possibly even informal guidance from the judge, indicating that the family court couldn't address the criminal allegations in the defendant's objections. Consequently, the defendant reported me to the police for alleged criminal behavior after submitting her objections in the case.

This situation arose from the defendant's inadequate representation. The legal representative, a family lawyer, typically takes client statements at face value without independent investigation. While misrepresenting feelings in a family case might be overlooked, false criminal accusations are grave. The limited scope of legal practice in Germany, combined with a lifetime of adhering strictly to specific procedures, led this lawyer to misinterpret criminal actions under family law. She based her case solely on the defendant's narrative without verifying its authenticity. This oversight made her an unwitting accomplice in perjury, and I suspect her active implication on the fabricated evidence.

Fabricating proves or/and perjury isn't this for a lawyer a reason to get warning from the lawyer's association bar?

Considering the law as a global entity, as soon everywhere in the developed world main principles are alike, I consider taking into consideration for improving any law system, cases, facts and practices from any court in any developed place.

On my own, having base knowledge and experience in a few jurisdictions, I can't consider any jurisdiction as perfect or without problems, but any system has elements that are unique and work well serving justice.

Failing to compare jurisdiction means isolation and non-improvement of a living virtue as is justice, despite that justice is the whole virtue (Aristoteles, The Art of Rhetoric)

Family court cases are often perceived by the global community as intricate legal matters, spanning multiple areas of law.

For instance, Australia's Family Law Act of 1975 encompasses sections that address criminal behaviors within the purview of family court proceedings. But the criminal facts are not proceeded with by the family court, as happens in any other place. Australian law also separates criminal and family cases and lets the criminal allegations proceed through a criminal court. Australian family law, when criminal behavior occurs within the context of family law cases, such as domestic violence or child abuse, these actions are typically addressed in different jurisdictions like a Magistrates' Court or higher criminal court.

Family law matters are usually handled in the Family Court or Federal Circuit Court. When criminal acts occur, these may be prosecuted under criminal law in separate courts. In family court proceedings, issues of family violence are particularly significant as they impact decisions, especially regarding parenting orders. Courts prioritize protecting children from harm, and evidence of family violence or child abuse plays a crucial role in these decisions.

The Family Court can issue injunctions for personal protection, and breaching these can lead to criminal charges. Additionally, affected parties can seek intervention orders in local or state courts. There is an indirect interaction between family and criminal courts, where outcomes of criminal cases can influence family court decisions, particularly concerning children's welfare.

Given these complexities and the serious implications of criminal allegations in family law matters, individuals are advised to seek legal representation to navigate the legal frameworks, protect rights and interests, and understand the consequences of criminal conduct in family law disputes. There are also legislative systems that do not specifically link criminal acts directly to family law. Instead, they either remain open-ended or have distinct rules that associate criminal allegations or elements from other legal areas with family law.

Germany, on the other hand, has confined family cases within a very restrictive legal framework, opting to disregard any subsequent legal issues that may arise during proceedings.

In the current case, two primary allegations were entirely overlooked by the court. Firstly, there were criminal allegations made by the mother. Even though a police investigation was conducted, and a report was produced that debunked these allegations, this evidence was not incorporated into the court's records. Secondly, the matter of citizenship, which was extensively debated during the hearing, was wholly dismissed by the court. in fact, the judge in a dramatic outburst, in order to keep the case within the framework of family law to avoid any involvement with further matters, overtly demonstrated, as previously described, an act of populism, making it unmistakably clear without any subtlety. Anyhow, this raises a pertinent question for the German family court: Is an intentional delay in the citizenship process, as alleged by the mother, or a negligent one, as I contend, viewed as child neglect? If it isn't, then why does the authorities intervene when there's a delay in children obtaining citizenship?

The entire court process spanned over three years, focusing solely on family law issues. Had the court genuinely begun to address all these allegations — pausing proceedings to allow for police investigations or to seek clarity on the children's immigration status — the process would likely have taken twice as long. Particularly concerning immigration status, there's a lack of authoritative entities capable of elucidating the exact nature of the problem in court. Given these conditions, the speed at which the proceedings unfolded was indeed advantageous.

Criminal allegations

During my custody case hearings, the criminal actions of my legal opponent were scarcely referenced, another option from a Family court couldn't require. However, what about the actual criminal acts committed during the court proceedings themselves? Even when these real-time offenses were brought up in one of the hearings, the judge showed disdain, indeed, but made no effort to understand the allegations.

Of course, it is not within the family judge's functions to adjudicate a criminal case during a family court hearing. The suggestion to suspend the family case for the duration of the criminal proceedings is quite unusual in the context of family court. Therefore, I understand why the judge would hesitate to initiate such an action.

Despite having a highly competent lawyer who excelled in her field of family law, the notion of requesting a hold on the family case was extremely unusual. It was an unprecedented tactic. Therefore, my request did not garner her support.

Under such circumstances, this case could be deemed an exception. The occurrence of criminal acts within a family case, coupled with the request to pause proceedings until the resolution of the criminal case, is rather unusual in family law. However, modern Civil law rarely accepts exceptions, necessitating the case to proceed as if there were no anomalies. The judge simply disregarded the criminal aspect, failed to summon third parties affected by the impending decision, and this behavior was accepted by all parties involved. They strictly followed the formal procedure. Even the police overlooked calls regarding blatant deception, dismissed evidence and my testimony, simply because the system is not structured in that way to examine a criminal case while pausing a family law proceeding.

Third-party notice

In German legal proceedings, such as in family court cases, third-party involvement, known as "Streitverkündung" (third-party notice) or

"Nebenintervention" (third-party intervention/joinder), is a common aspect, guided by the Zivilprozessordnung (ZPO), the German Code of Civil Procedure. While third-party involvement usually originates from one of the lawsuit's parties, the court may sometimes find it necessary to involve a third party, such as the immigration office in cases related to immigration issues.

Despite the potential relevance of third-party involvement, there have been instances where the court has not overruled any statement, objection, or allegation concerning the immigration matter, strategically avoiding the immigration issue's integration into the case. This approach suggests a deliberate decision to sideline certain aspects, potentially impacting the case's comprehensive and fair resolution. If the court considers it necessary to involve the immigration office in the hearing, the court may order a mandatory subpoena. The integration or exclusion of such third-party entities can significantly influence the case's outcome, highlighting the importance of judicial discretion in these matters.

Bias under German law

The term "Voreingenommenheit," which translates to "bias" or "prejudice" in German, can be found in various aspects of German law, particularly in the context of administrative law and criminal law.

The term "Voreingenommenheit" (bias or prejudice) can also be relevant in the context of German family law, particularly in cases involving family court proceedings or disputes related to family matters. While the term itself may not be explicitly mentioned in the family law statutes, the concept of impartiality and the avoidance of bias are fundamental principles that apply across various areas of law, including family law.

In family law proceedings, such as divorce, child custody, spousal support, and child support cases, it is essential that judges and other relevant authorities approach cases with objectivity and without bias. If there are concerns about the impartiality of a judge or decision-maker in a family law case, parties involved may have mechanisms to address such concerns.

While the term "Voreingenommenheit" itself may not be explicitly used in family law statutes, the principle of impartiality and the avoidance of bias are essential in ensuring fair and just outcomes in family law matters. The specific procedures and mechanisms for addressing bias concerns in family law cases may be outlined in procedural rules and regulations that apply to family court proceedings.

In Australian family law, the term "bias" is relevant in the context of ensuring fair and impartial proceedings in family law matters. Like in many legal systems, maintaining impartiality and avoiding bias is essential to uphold the principles of justice and fairness in family law cases. However, the specific use of the term "bias" may not be explicitly mentioned in Australian family law statutes.

Instead, the principles of fairness, impartiality, and avoiding bias are embedded in the broader framework of family law legislation and rules. Key aspects where these principles are applicable in Australian family law include:

Family Law Act 1975: The Family Law Act 1975 is the primary legislation governing family law matters in Australia. While the Act may not use the term "bias" explicitly, it does outline principles related to the welfare and best interests of children, property division, and other matters. The Act emphasizes the importance of impartial decision-making to achieve just outcomes.

Judicial Impartiality: Family law matters are heard in family law courts, including the Family Court of Australia and the Federal Circuit Court of Australia. The judiciary in these courts is expected to adhere to principles of judicial impartiality and fairness when handling family law cases.

Professional Conduct Rules: Legal practitioners in Australia are subject to professional conduct rules, including those related to family law matters. These rules require lawyers to act in the best interests of their clients while maintaining professionalism and ethical conduct, which includes not exhibiting bias.

Complaints and Appeals: Parties involved in family law cases have mechanisms to address concerns related to bias. They can seek remedies through appeals, complaints, or seeking the recusal of a judge or decision-maker if they believe bias has affected their case.

While the term "bias" may not be explicitly mentioned in Australian family law statutes, the principles of fairness, impartiality, and the avoidance of bias are fundamental to the administration of justice in family law matters. Legal professionals and the judiciary are expected to uphold these principles to ensure equitable outcomes for all parties involved in family law cases.

Bias, whether in the context of common law or in specific jurisdictions, is a fundamental concern in legal proceedings to ensure fairness and impartiality.

In the common law system, which is followed in countries like the United States, Canada, the United Kingdom, Hong Kong and Cyprus, the principle of avoiding bias and ensuring impartiality is essential.

Common law jurisdictions have developed a body of case law and legal standards that address issues related to bias. Judges are expected to recuse themselves from cases if they have a conflict of interest or if there is a reasonable apprehension of bias.

Parties to legal proceedings can seek remedies if they believe that bias has affected their case. They may request a judge's recusal or appeal a decision if they believe that the proceedings were tainted by bias or a lack of impartiality.

While any Family Code may not explicitly mention the term "bias" in the context of family law, the principles of fairness and impartiality are fundamental in family law proceedings. Judges and other decision-makers are expected to handle family law cases objectively and without prejudice.

Common is that principles of impartiality and fairness are vital in family law matters. Parties have avenues to address concerns about bias or a lack of impartiality within the legal framework. Legal practitioners and judicial authorities are expected to uphold these principles to ensure just outcomes in family law cases.

Competence Conflict

In Germany, provisional decisions in family law matters, particularly those involving children, are typically handled by the Youth Welfare Office (Jugendamt). The

Youth Welfare Office, although a government institution, does not necessarily require its decision-makers to have formal legal qualifications. This approach prioritizes social welfare perspectives over legal expertise in making decisions that affect children's lives.

In contrast, Greece mandates that such provisional decisions must be made by judicial institutions, specifically the courts or, in urgent situations, by the prosecutor. This system ensures that decisions are always made by individuals or bodies with legal qualifications and training. The key distinction lies not in the timeliness of the decisions but in the nature of the decision-making body. While Germany delegates these responsibilities to a social welfare institution, Greece entrusts them solely to legally trained professionals or judicial authorities.

This difference highlights a fundamental divergence in the approach to family law between the two countries: Germany incorporates a social welfare perspective, while Greece adheres strictly to a legalistic approach.

The beauty of the law lies in its limitless possibilities for interpretation, especially in multifaceted cases like the one I'm referencing. There are countless ways to interpret and apply the law. In my situation, the German legal system handled the case in a manner less favorable to the children. These children have faced citizenship issues since birth, and the recent decision hasn't ameliorated these challenges. Although the citizenship issue was raised multiple times during the hearing and used by both parties to bolster their claims, the judge, police, and other authorities chose not to delve into it. Evidence suggests that at least the eldest child was brought to Germany illegally, making her a victim. This victim status could implicate the mother, third parties, or both. However, recognizing the children as a victim could grant them privileges typically reserved for refugees. Including identity problem solving!

Family law cases are often implicating multiple areas of law like when parents from different countries are divorcing, and there are disputes about which country the child should reside in. This could involve:

Family Law: For the custody arrangement.
International Law: For determining jurisdiction and applicable law.
Immigration Law: If one of the parents or the child is not a citizen of the country where the case is being heard.

Criminal Law: If there are allegations of abuse or other criminal conduct by one of the parents.

Family court cases are often perceived by the global community as intricate legal matters, spanning multiple areas of law.

For instance, Australia's Family Law Act of 1975 encompasses sections that address criminal behaviors within the purview of family court proceedings. However, there are also legislations that do not specifically link criminal acts directly to family law. Instead, they either remain open-ended or have distinct rules that associate criminal allegations or elements from other legal areas with family law.

Germany, on the other hand, has confined family cases within a very restrictive legal framework, opting to disregard any subsequent legal issues that may arise during proceedings.

Reconciliation

The German civil legal system, generally and specifically on family matters, aims to find mutually acceptable resolutions, adhering to the principle that there are no definitive winners or losers but rather a collectively agreed-upon solution. That is understandable in family cases, indeed, but the current case is an exceptionally challenging case, the court seeks reconciliation even as the situation verges on criminal prosecution.

Despite the currently positive relationship with my children's mother, marked by regular visits and communication, and our ability to handle matters concerning our children maturely, calmly, and harmoniously, I often ponder how we reached this point of reconciliation. Particularly, I reflect on how I successfully navigated rebuilding trust with someone who previously made false accusations against me for horrible crimes I never committed. How did we achieve such a successful turnaround?

This situation isn't attributed to the court's merits; quite the contrary, the court and other involved parties totally refused to offer genuine assistance to the defendant.

The mother seemed unaware of the situation's gravity and unable to express her own free will. I doubt her mental or intellectual capacity to fabricate a story and file a denunciation against me with the police. It appears that even those who may have influenced her lack the capability. Certain instances from the court hearings shed light on what I mean.

Following the preparation of the expert report, which proposed that the children be raised in a government facility located far from the town with minimal visitation rights for the parents, the report was submitted to the court. Subsequently, the parties involved were required to declare their acceptance or rejection of the recommendation.

Regarding the expert's suggested solution, the court assistant approved it, while the youth welfare office and I rejected it. The defendant's solicitor requested a five-minute break to discuss the situation with her client. However, this break was extended to an unexpected 30 minutes. After this prolonged pause, the defendant finally declared her readiness to respond. Surprisingly, she agreed in court to relinquish her custodial rights entirely, consenting to have the children raised in a government facility.

At that moment, the youth welfare office suggested external therapy at a reputable facility or with a recognized doctor for the children to support their developmental process, recommending that the children continue to reside with their father.

On my part, I agreed to the youth welfare office's suggestion for outpatient therapy. Additionally, I affirmed my intention to stay in Germany, and requested that the youth welfare office support my parenting by implementing ongoing family social assistance at my home. This would involve a social worker visiting at least twice a week to monitor the children's living environment and behavioral development, for at least the next 2 years and then reporting their observations to both the court and the youth welfare office about every three months.

Three or four months later, the first report from the experienced social worker became the turning point. It led the court and the involved parties to reject the expert's proposed solution. The expert then withdrew her recommendation and concurred with the children staying with their father. The court assistant also amended her stance, requesting a restricted order to prevent me and the children leaving Frankfurt.

Let's revisit the moment at the hearing of the extended pause requested by the defendant's first lawyer to clarify to her client the expert's report and the request for the children to grow up in a government facility. After that day's hearing concluded, I approached the defendant to meet a few hours later. My intention was to understand her mindset in voluntarily relinquishing her children, considering the repercussions this decision could have on her future interactions with them. Additionally, I was concerned about the impact on the children, who would be placed in a government facility for the second time, experiencing the trauma all over again. This time, the situation seemed even worse, with the potential for more significant changes like switching school or kindergarten. Furthermore, I explained how this development might affect her own immigration status.

I articulate and substantiate my assertions, aiming to persuade her to reconsider accepting the Expert's solution. This was necessary because, according to her account, her lawyer had not informed her of the full implications. She was under the impression that agreeing to the Expert's proposal was the path to regaining her children and that it would have no adverse effects on her immigration status.

Subsequently, she switched her legal representation to a more competent lawyer who could genuinely represent her real interests. This new attorney had the professional capability to align with her actual desires. She then reversed her earlier acceptance of the Expert's proposal, rejecting it outright. Additionally, she eliminated the unreliable witness from her defense strategy and, crucially, prioritized the protection of her immigration status in a transparent and focused manner.

De Facto / de Jure

From the start of the court procedure, the defendant has had a complex immigration status. She was on a permitted stay pending deportation, receiving extensions every six months. This status allowed many people to remain in Germany for extended periods, even though the state did not officially accept them, excluding them from benefits typically guaranteed in Europe. Practically, these people are located in Germany; theoretically, they are not. It is precisely here that the legal terms "de jure" and "de facto" apply to the current case.

In fact, the defendant utilized her immigration status extremely effectively. Even when there were accusations against her, the police could not take further action. The issue is that, de facto, the defendant resides in Germany, but de jure, she is not officially recognized anywhere. And here exactly starts the legal problem of the children's Citizenship, because their mother can't prove her de jure existence by failing to submit a valuable birth and/or family certificate.

The situation is legally complex. Initially, the court cannot verify the litigants' legal status and identity. Due to time constraints, family court procedures, which are typically expedited, could not delve into these legal details. As a preliminary measure, the court did not investigate deeply but chose to follow a standard procedure, oversimplifying a highly unusual case. This raises the question: How many other cases are German courts handling with specific adjustments, following a pattern while ignoring critical elements and facts, especially under family law? Effectively, the German court system needs to initiate multiple independent cases to thoroughly examine this scenario. How would independent decisions from different courts affect each other? For instance, if a criminal case identified me as abusive or dangerous, wouldn't that lead to a change in the custody decision? Or, if I were to challenge the defendant's legal competence, wouldn't that prompt the court to alter the current custody arrangement?

The primary concern in all these scenarios is time. Indeed, Germany handles matters maturely, or at least that is the belief of the German legal system. However, the processing of these matters is notably slow.

Lawyers compared

In Germany, under the civil law system, lawyers are primarily advocates and advisors for their clients. They meticulously prepare their cases based on written laws and statutes. They interpret the complex body of written laws and explain how they apply to their client's situation. They represent clients in negotiations and court, putting forward arguments, submitting evidence, and ensuring adherence to procedural rules. A lot of emphasis is placed on written submissions and precise documentation, as judgments are often based on these documents.

In common law countries, lawyers also advise and advocate but in different ways, they spend considerable time researching past judicial decisions relevant to their case, as these precedents can heavily influence the outcome. They often have more in-court presence, especially in higher-level courts, where they present oral arguments, cross-examine witnesses, and argue motions. Outside of court, they might spend more time negotiating settlements or agreements, as there's often more room for flexibility compared to civil law systems.

In both systems, the lawyer's ultimate goal is to serve the client's best interests, but the strategies and methods they use can vary significantly due to the underlying legal processes and traditions.

Lawyers in Germany and in other jurisdictions

In the German civil law system, lawyers focus a lot on written laws. They help clients understand these laws and how they apply to their situations. Their work often involves a lot of paperwork, and they must be very precise. They argue cases in court too, but it's really important how they prepare their documents.

In common law countries, like the U.S. or the U.K., lawyers do things a bit differently. They look at decisions from past cases because those can affect current cases. They're also active in court, questioning witnesses and making arguments. They often try to settle things outside of court as well.

So, while lawyers in both systems are there to help their clients, the way they do it can be quite different because of how the two legal systems work.

Practicing in Scandinavian countries involves different approaches, primarily due to the variations in legal systems and cultural influences.

Scandinavian countries (like Sweden, Denmark, and Norway) have legal systems that are often considered to be a mix of civil law and common law traditions, though they lean more towards civil law. The role of a lawyer, or "advokat," in these countries is somewhat different. The legal culture in Scandinavian countries tends to be less formal. There's a strong emphasis on negotiation and mediation, with lawyers often engaging in collaborative discussions to resolve disputes outside of courtrooms. Lawyers might have broader practice, dealing with a range of legal matters since there's a tradition of generalism in some of these countries. While they also rely on written submissions, there might be more room for oral advocacy in a less rigid style compared to German practice. The court proceedings could be more interactive. Scandinavian legal practices also reflect the high level of social trust in these societies. There's a significant focus on welfare and social justice, which can influence legal outcomes.

East Europe countries tend to have a mix of civil and case law system. Lawyers who mostly build their cases based on the written laws but often use past cases on the preparation of their cases. The big difference is in how exactly the case is developed in the courtroom and what exactly the role of the lawyers.

Civil cases in those court rooms are developing in the form of a trial, with open statements, witness/litigants direct and cross examination, conclusions or closing arguments and final decision.

Arguments and proofs are carefully prepared by the lawyers who are obligated to have clear proof for any argument or answer. Arguments or statements not based on reasonable proof may easily be considered speculative and will be eliminated immediately. Mostly that kind of intervention happens through the opposite lawyer, but in very extreme situations also the judge may intervene. Building a case as a lawyer in such a system must be very carefully structured and have to be based on laws and real proofs. Of course, all the preparation of paperwork, preparation of witnesses, before the deadline submissions and the responsibility for making a favorable decision rest exclusively with the lawyer.

As I already mentioned, I don't find any law system perfect. There are plenty of cons as well as plenty pros in any system. Having such a flexible system as happen in Eastern Europe doesn't mean that it's a fair system at all, there are a lot of manipulations tricks according to the scope of the lawyer, but what system doesn't have those kinds of lawyers, who try to use the law beyond the norm of justice. That's why there is the bar association, which carefully investigates cases of abusive or manipulative members, and ensures the disbarment of any rules breaker.

The association Bar functions are extremely necessary, and its existence is fully understandable for places like East Europe or for common law countries, as the law is very flexible the situation may escape control and harm the trust of the people on the legal function of their own system. So, the Bar association is informed if lawyers get criminal record which will cause the loss of lawyer license or more often, lawyers become a warning for unethical behavior. Unethical behavior that may cause disbarment are also fabrications of evidence.

The Bar association is less strict in places like Germany where the law business is covered by trustful professionals who have too little space to move, making it for them less likely to take an unethical or out of norms path.

Under these circumstances seems like the Bar association in Germany exists only as one more decorative institution where people work there instead of being unemployed, as many work position in Germany have this kind of scope. Of course, is rising the question who should denunciate the unethical behavior at the Bar, which in the current case this action primary rests one more time with the judge

Greek Ombudsman (Synigoros tou politi)

Upon recognizing my first daughter and identifying the legal issues with the mother's identity, after first attempting to solve the case through the registrar of the registry office in Greece, I approached the Greek Ombudsman (Synigoros tou politi) for a resolution, leveraging the defendant's granted asylum status.

My argument was straightforward: asylum seekers, persecuted or discriminated against in their home countries for reasons like religion, political beliefs, or sexual orientation, cannot safely obtain identity documents from those very countries. Recognizing this, the asylum institution acknowledged the improbability of the mother providing necessary identity proofs from her country of origin. The law grants asylum seekers residency in a host country, permitting free movement everywhere but their country of origin. This principle is foundational, aiming to protect individuals from the very dangers they fled. Therefore, expecting these individuals to obtain identity documents from their home countries contradicts the essence of asylum — it's both impractical and potentially jeopardizes their safety. Requesting such documents could, in fact, undermine the validity of their asylum status, indicating a flawed interpretation of asylum laws. Asylum grants individuals a fresh start, independent of their previous life and status, and the legal framework should consistently reflect this understanding.

Despite lengthy correspondence to Greek Ombudsman (Synigoros tou politi) and initial rejections while I was in Germany, the institution eventually granted a decision that enabled my daughter to acquire Greek citizenship without the mother's identity verification. This decision opened a pathway for the mother to secure a permanent European residency through her daughter's Greek citizenship. Contradictorily, she chose to leave Greece and travel illegally to Germany with our daughter, who then lacked any citizenship. This action not only jeopardized our daughter's opportunity for Greek citizenship but also her chances for a stable European residency, which remains her primary concern and furthermore, her move to Germany caused the loss of her asylum status.

This bewildering move raises profound questions. She abandoned a secure route to European residency, claiming it was the only way to save her life. This behavior invites speculation: Is she evading local law enforcement, or does she suffer from a serious psychological issue? My attempt to clarify this through a European criminal record request, especially under her previous name before moving to Germany, as she change her name after arriving, but this my request was unsupported by authorities.

Should the criminal record return clean, her mental health becomes the focal point. Even if she fears criminal associations, her actions are inexplicably risky. Neither the police nor the court, responsible for assessing parental fitness, have uncovered her motivations.

Would the court have approached the case differently had she sought more substantial parental rights or custody? Her perplexing decisions leave us with more questions than answers about her intentions and the legal system's response to such complex cases.

Roman law history

As previously mentioned, every country has laws and procedures designed to foster harmonious living, tailored to the realities of daily life. Each legal system contributes to the broader pursuit of justice, and the German legal system is no exception. Rooted in Roman law, the German system, like many others worldwide, is built on a structured framework of written statutes that aim to serve justice.

The Roman law itself evolved over a millennium, absorbing and studying the laws and customs of the territories it conquered. In its early history, Roman justice often applied the laws of an immigrant's homeland for crimes they committed on Roman soil. The development of Roman law was a comprehensive exercise in comparative law, enriched by a deep dive into the knowledge and ideas of other cultures.

Law is indeed an evolving entity, continually adapting to the times and the needs of society. However, merely adjusting existing laws isn't sufficient; true progress requires fundamental changes at the law's very core.

I envision a future where the Roman law system incorporates a permanent, exceptional court. This court would consist of a judicial panel of at least three judges and possibly a procurator, tasked with adjudicating cases upon the request of one or both parties involved.

Judgments issued by this court could serve as a foundational reference for the evolution of statutory law or for substantial reforms in the core of the relevant legislation

The law in each place is an always developing entity, developed and adjusted from and for the people on which it is applied.

Comparative law, in the time I studied in the faculty of justice (Class 2004) the lesson of the Comparative law was voluntary,

It's a fact that family matters and criminal matters are handled separately in all western jurisdictions, but the connection to each other seems to be handled differently in each place. It seems that there're even jurisdictions that give a specific function to the family court about how to handle the existence of open criminal dispute while deciding on a family matter.

Zeungger Case

The Zaunegger case, involving a father seeking joint custody for his daughter born out of wedlock. Tragically,

Zaunegger was dismissed at every level of the German judicial system, culminating in a final appeal to the European Court of Human Rights. Justice was indeed served there, but a glance at the timeline reveals a distressing fact: the case was initiated when his daughter was merely 3 years old and concluded just before her 18th birthday. This is an unfortunate mark against justice. Zaunegger's case holds significant importance for single fathers in Germany post-2010, we owe him a debt of gratitude. Quite simply, Zaunegger pursued his case to the European Court not for his own sake – he was aware his personal battle was over – but to challenge and change the German stereotype favoring female exclusivity in parenthood. My respect goes out to Mr. Zaunegger for his dedication and perseverance.

Stefan Zweig

Stefan Zweig's renowned novel, the "Schachnovelle" or "Chess Novella", delves into the story of an intellectual individual imprisoned during wartime. He finds himself with only a stolen chess book hidden in his cell for reading material. With nothing else to engage his mind, he turns to the book, learning the game of chess.

Upon gaining his freedom, he tries his hand at chess and discovers that the game isn't just about following rules -

it's about understanding them. The protagonist internalizes specific moves, positions, and patterns from the book, only to realize that these patterns don't apply identically in real-world scenarios.

This story serves as a metaphor for our understanding of law, codes, or the constitution. These guidelines help shape our perception of justice but leave room for interpretation depending on the case at hand. No single book can predict all possible solutions or scenarios, as highlighted by Aristoteles. Viewing a case through a narrow scope of law, while ignoring its broader context, can result in justice being shortchanged.

This misinterpretation often occurs due to bias. Legal practitioners may become accustomed to interpreting certain cases in a specific way, applying a rigid pattern and forgetting that the application and interpretation of the law should be limitless.

It's concerning to see biases manifest, such as in Germany, where a family matter case was suspended due to criminal acts. It's understandable that these are separate legal domains, but neglecting additional interventions or ignoring pertinent facts simply because family law cases are typically processed in a certain way is a restrictive stereotype.

My case in other jurisdictions

The outcome of custody battles is highly sensitive to the specific circumstances of each case, including detailed considerations that haven't occurred in the current case. Based on general principles and important considerations in the context of the legal systems in various countries, family law is a complex field that can vary significantly even within regions of the same country. The details provided would all be seriously negative for the mother's case in any jurisdiction, but they would be investigated and considered in detail.

United Kingdom: In the UK, child welfare is also the court's paramount concern. The court would consider reports from social services and possibly appoint a separate legal representative for the children (a guardian ad litem). The mother's criminal activities, especially violence in front of the children, and dishonesty related to legal proceedings, would count heavily against her. The UK courts would look very critically at any parent using children for immigration purposes. If the father can provide a safe and stable environment, he might be granted residency or full custody.

Australia: Australian courts prioritize the best interests of the child, with an emphasis on protecting them from harm. The mother's history of violence and instability, along with her legal transgressions, would be severe strikes against her. Australia also recognizes the importance of children having a relationship with both parents, but this is balanced against the need to keep them safe. The father could be granted sole custody if the mother is deemed a risk, and she might get supervised visitation rights, depending on the circumstances.

United States: In the U.S., laws vary by state, but all prioritize the best interests of the children. The court would consider each parent's ability to provide a stable, nurturing environment. The mother's criminal behavior, particularly involving violence and dishonesty, would seriously undermine her case. Using children as tools for immigration status would also likely be frowned upon. Custody arrangements in the U.S. are often designed to ensure continued relationships with both parents, but if one parent is deemed unfit or dangerous, the other could be awarded full custody.

Greece: Like in other countries, Greek family law focuses on the child's best interests. The court would take into account all relevant factors, including the parental capacity of both parents, the children's emotional ties to each parent, and the parents' ability to provide for the children's needs. The mother's criminal record, perjury, and exploitation of the children for residency purposes would weigh heavily against her. Greek law acknowledges the importance of family unity, but not at the expense of the children's safety and well-being. The father could be granted custody, with the mother potentially receiving some form of access or visitation rights, under supervision if necessary.

In all these jurisdictions, the courts would require comprehensive assessments, often involving social workers or psychological experts, especially given the severity of the mother's actions. It's also worth noting that in many of these countries, there is an increasing emphasis on mediation and collaborative decision-making in family law cases, encouraging parents to come to an agreement outside of court when possible. However, in severe situations like the current one, judicial intervention becomes necessary.

Taking in consideration Aristoteles

Considering Aristotle's contributions to the modern justice system, it is acknowledged that there are two sides to every case: the just and the unjust. As the history of justice evolved, a clear division of cases into criminal and civil categories emerged, followed by even more granular categorizations.

In terms of procedure, many systems handle cases similarly—through trials that include testimonies, witness examination, cross-examination, and then a verdict, applicable to both criminal and civil cases.

Scandinavian and, to an extent, German law, aim not solely to discern fair from unfair in civil disputes, but rather to seek a mutually acceptable resolution.

This approach is indeed revolutionary and innovative, though it may not always align with traditional notions of justice. In complex family matters, such as divorce, child custody, or alimony, which may involve intricate issues like adultery or serious crimes, finding a consensus can be challenging, if not unfeasible.

Nevertheless, courts often strive to confine these cases within the boundaries of family law, at times disregarding extraneous arguments. The German legal system, in particular, is adept at excluding considerations beyond the immediate scope, such as those related to immigration or criminal allegations. This exclusion is not due to oversight or neglect during proceedings; rather, it's a deliberate feature of the legal framework, and this intentional creation of legal gaps is, arguably, the most troubling aspect.

Substantive Trial - Constitutionality

In the German legal system, trials on the merits typically occur at the first instance courts, which are primarily responsible for fact-finding and applying the law to those facts.

Decisions from first instance courts can typically be appealed to higher courts. The appellate courts (Oberlandesgerichte) review cases from the regional courts, focusing more on legal errors than on fact-finding.

The Federal Court of Justice (Bundesgerichtshof) is the highest court for civil and criminal matters, primarily dealing with legal questions of fundamental significance and ensuring uniform application of the law.

It's important to note that the approach of German appellate courts is quite different from that in some common law jurisdictions, where appellate courts may have broader scope for re-hearing cases on both facts and law.

Indirectly I'm excluded from the right to appeal against this. I can't leave my children any longer without citizenship, for legal and for moral reasons. But I cannot raise concerns about the constitutionality of the procedure without prior examination of all court levels.

There is this procedure of postponed appeal[4], but such a procedure would cost extreme long time is it really worth

---

[4] The legal term "postponed appeal" generally refers to a situation in legal proceedings where an appeal against a decision is deferred or delayed until a later point in time. This concept can manifest differently depending on the jurisdiction and the specific legal context in which it's applied. The underlying principle is that, under certain conditions, the right to appeal a decision or judgment is not exercised immediately after the decision is made but is instead reserved for a future

it? And is there any legal representation in Germany who could do that?

Legal Objections

Considering the foundational principles of the German legal system, which prioritize reaching mutually acceptable solutions, and acknowledging the rule that a case may only be tried on its merits in the first instance, it appears that my case is effectively concluded. The prospect of an appeal, under these circumstances, is unlikely to yield a favorable decision. Allow me to elaborate:

The core legal issues in this decision are rooted in the systemic framework of the law, which, unfortunately, are not subject to appeal. Moreover, the procedural aspects that might form the basis of an appeal would likely result in a mere repetition of the process in the first instance, with a new judge, court staff, and potentially a new expert psychologist. However, this does not guarantee consideration of crucial aspects such as immigration issues or the criminal elements of the case. Specifically, whether the citizenship status of the children could be reconsidered, or whether a parent's delay in securing

_____

date.

citizenship for the children constitutes neglect, remains uncertain.

Furthermore, my request for the court to incorporate the police investigation report into the case file, or my grievance regarding the court's failure to assess the defendant's state of mind during the commission of violent acts in the presence of the children, addresses the substantive merits of the case. These are aspects that an appellate court is not empowered to examine. Additionally, my objections to the merits of the applicable law itself are beyond the scope of remedial action in this context.

At the heart of this case are the children. The situation is unique in that there was no divorce or significant misunderstanding between the parents. Under these circumstances, the involvement of the youth welfare office and the court assistant was intended for one specific purpose: to represent the children's rights. Regrettably, a significant portion of the proceedings, particularly the defendant's statements, lacks any consideration of the children's rights or interests

Court Assistant

The court assistant is an institution aimed at protecting the rights of minors. Unlike the youth welfare office and the expert, the court assistant is responsible for meeting with the children or visiting their place of residence.

However, in my case, this never occurred, which initially did not present a problem. The issue arose when the court assistant began actively investigating the defendant's false claims after the police investigation had concluded. She started submitting reports to the court, attempting to undermine my position further. This led to the intervention of the youth welfare office, which highlighted that the court assistant had failed to perform her duties, such as meeting with the children or assessing their living conditions and had never met the plaintiff in person.

Furthermore, the court assistant is a well-paid institution with apparent connections to the defendant's witness. She confidently declared in the courtroom, during a hearing, that she knew the witness, had met with them, and even used the witness as a translator during meetings with the defendant. Regrettably, in the family court, there was no third-party record keeper; records were maintained via a recording device controlled by the judge. The primary concern was not that the court assistant used the witness as a translator or her prior contact with the witness, but her brazen confidence in openly discussing these facts in court, even off the record, without facing any consequences. Finally, the court assistant expressed her support for the expert's report and agreed with the decision for the children to grow up in an institution separate from their parents.

The Expert

This institution also try to play a roll of an investigator, as is common understandable the criminal accusations of the defendant were that furious that made anyone worrying, that finally was the defendants target, the most astonishing on this behavior wasn't exactly the initiative to request clarification about this case from me instead of asking the court, but she openly expressed this her behavior in her report that she submitted to the court. I mean she wrote openly on the report that she asked for clarification and also some proves from me, before starting the interview for her report.

Self the report is not exactly a deep examination of the situation of the attendees, this is accepted, considering that the whole procedure for getting a result is kept as short as possible serving the custody case all this is accepted. Psychological evolution should mostly be able to recognize signs of risky behaviors, consumption of illegal or dangerous substances and generally emergency situations that may occur during the child's care. A psychologist in such a function is more capable to result on possible problems instead of clear results as they are looking for patterns to put their subjects on a specific category and come up with a result which in fact is based on hypotheses instead of facts. And it is really astonishing that a psychologist took the initiative to start an investigation into criminal behavior but never asked or made any investigation about psychological facts.

Considering that the specific psychological institution is one of the most famous institutions in the country and the head and founder of the institution is a highly respected person in the country who expresses himself openly in the media. Mostly after the refugees' crises of 2015, her believe of the necessity all the children coming from problematic families or difficult places to have part of their life pasted in government psychological faculties for a couple of years or of their whole childhood. And this is something that, seams, common accepted in Germany.

The defendant's first lawyer

In civil cases, a lawyer's focus is primarily on advocating for their client's interests. This contrasts with criminal cases, where a lawyer must leverage all available evidence and legal strategies to secure the best possible outcome for their client. A notable issue in the current case was a clear communication breakdown between the lawyer and her client, leading to the client's genuine requests being omitted from her legal statements.

Surprisingly, the defense strategy seemed to align with the expert's viewpoint favoring children being raised in institutional settings over familial care. This alignment was peculiar, especially since the statements failed to address the mother's willingness to participate in her children's upbringing or her preferences regarding contact frequency with them, aside from a single verbal request for phone communication during the hearing.

Moreover, the lawyer's strategy aggressively questioned my parenting capabilities without leaving room for an anticipated objection based on speculation. Despite my explicit desire to introduce the defendant's European Criminal Record into the proceedings—a move I could not initiate due to the mother not seeking any form of custody—this angle was not pursued.

Even the defendant's second lawyer, who displayed better client communication and a more professional demeanor, did not seek custody or visitation rights but focused solely on securing her client's residency in Germany on behalf of the children.

This approach raises questions about the initial lawyer's professionalism and the need for regulatory bodies to address such conduct. How prevalent are such practices among legal professionals, and what mechanisms exist to mitigate these issues without resulting in repercussions?

The Judges

In legal proceedings, irrespective of the jurisdiction, the principle of judicial sovereignty is fundamental. The scope of a judge's authority may vary across different legal systems, yet the essence of judicial responsibility remains central. Specifically, in the German legal framework, where judges possess extensive competencies, it falls upon them to challenge any speculative statements made by litigants, particularly when such statements lack crucial elements. In this case, the defendant's failure to contest my petition for sole custody or to demonstrate an intention to reclaim custodial rights—or even to articulate her capacity and willingness to contribute to the upbringing of the children—was noteworthy.

This matter was heard by a single judge, yet the unusual substitution of the judge introduced an additional layer of complexity. With the defendant's statements scrutinized by two different judges, one might infer that the acceptance of these statements by both judges signifies their compatibility with prevailing legal standards. However, neither judge pursued inquiries nor sought clarification regarding the evident contradictions and missing explanations within the defendant's narrative. Despite the defendant's lack of effort to regain custody or to clarify her objectives, especially under the stringent scrutiny of German law, one would anticipate the judge questioning the nature of the defendant's custodial aspirations.

The dilemma posed is intricate: advocating for joint custody would appear contradictory given her allegations of my criminality; seeking sole custody would necessitate substantiating her mental and emotional stability, as indicated by police records and recommendations from the youth welfare office—a process that could significantly delay decisions regarding the children's placement. Consequently, transferring temporary custody to the youth welfare office could inadvertently facilitate her deportation, a prospect she evidently feared. Opting to speculate in her statements rather than formally requesting custody rights, her approach was ultimately endorsed by the court and the judges involved.

Ground for Appel

The court's decision to grant both the defendant and the plaintiff mutual authority to determine the children's place of residence raises significant legal concerns. Specifically, the decision overlooks the fact that the mother lacks both a residence permit and a means of identification in the country. The legal basis for determining the children's country of residence remains unclear, especially given the ambiguity surrounding the mother's own place of residence. While aiming to preserve the mother-children relationship by allowing her to decide on their place of residence, the court's decision to specify the exact country and town exceeds its remit, essentially encroaching upon the domain of the immigration authorities by dictating the mother's residency.

Furthermore, this decision represents a clear conflict of competence. A family court should not determine the residency rights of the parties involved, including the children, without a clear request from those parties. Although the court assistant, who may lack comprehensive legal expertise, submitted, verbally, a request for the children to reside specifically in Germany and, more precisely, in Frankfurt, this request fails to articulate how such an arrangement serves the children's best interests.

The core responsibility of the court assistant is to safeguard the interests of the children. Hence, it is imperative to question how the court assistant justifies this request and how the court rationalizes its incorporation into its brief ruling. There are evident indicators that the court may have overstepped its jurisdiction, which necessitates a thorough examination in the appeal process to ensure that the decision aligns with the paramount interests of the children.

The Reform

The division and isolation of several legal areas can result in a limited understanding of justice. Any case can be impacted by any other law area case, and this is understandable only if we see the law connected between the different areas like communicating vessels. This constrained viewpoint makes it necessary for the legal representatives to work together on a case, making necessary the creation of multiple areas law offices or law firms, which is not intrinsically undesirable. However, when judges adopt such a constrained interpretation of the law, it creates an issue. This is especially true in family law issues, which can develop into extremely complicated situations involving numerous legal disciplines.

Within the rigorous framework of court systems, such as the one in Germany, distinct courts hear each unique matter. A significant point of inquiry is how a court addresses situations where it is tasked with examining allegations that actually pertain to another area of law and should ideally be evaluated by a different court.

In Germany, encountering allegations that fall outside the defined parameters of the law is extremely rare. Lawyers promptly represent their client's interests before the court once the requests are made. This representation becomes particularly crucial in cases like that of Mr. Zunegger, where an individual acts independently. Mr. Zunegger sought custody without legal representation, a move unheard of in Germany before 2010, as no lawyer would submit such a request. It was only when lodging a claim with the European Court of Human Rights that Mr. Zunegger first engaged a lawyer. In the initial and appellate levels, and even in the Supreme Court, the courts seemed to dismiss his request. Drawing from personal experience, it appears that judges may deliberately overlook criminal and immigration allegations, leveraging them to confine the case strictly within the boundaries of family law.

The law, when strictly confined to written rules, risks becoming an unjust tool that may favor some while excluding others. A legal system without provisions for exceptions or case-by-case examination threatens our freedom.

The Greek Ombudsman's proficient staff represents the sole entity with whom I could openly discuss and seek resolutions for my daughters' citizenship dilemma. This is because the individuals at the Ombudsman's office are specifically trained to devise solutions in situations where the law falls short. Such expertise is particularly necessary in our Roman law-based system, which requires adaptability to keep pace with rapid societal changes that outstrip the justice system's capacity to respond.

Beyond the children, the true casualty in this narrative is the mother, who remains deeply entrenched in African cultural beliefs, including the existence of ghosts and numerous spirits she perceives as constantly pursuing her. This scenario is deeply regrettable; both for the oversight of authorities who failed to understand her situation fully and for her personal plight. Migrating to Europe in hopes of escaping these 'ghosts,' she found a form of protection that ironically nobody ever told her, there aren't any ghosts.

Critical Examination

How can I regard Germany as a secure environment for raising my children when the system is governed by immutable laws, where lawyers face limitations, privileged individuals and institutions operate unchecked, and the police seemingly assess complaints selectively? This approach might be deemed tolerable due to Germany's large population and the prioritization of severe crimes. Similarly, doctors may prioritize serious health issues, and teachers might struggle to support students lacking sufficient intellectual encouragement from home.

In Germany, as in many other nations, exceptions are seldom made, acknowledging that some may be overlooked by the system. Comparable to a colonel who anticipates losses in battle, the legal system expects some individuals to fall through the cracks. The question is, how ready are we to be among those overlooked?

The case of "Genditzki" illustrates not only the wrongful conviction of an innocent person based on speculation but also the judiciary's prolonged 13 years to address his appeals. Upon release, he was offered compensation significantly less than he was entitled to through legal avenues, reminiscent of under-the-table dealings akin to those employed by the mafia to influence the state. This echoes the situation with Mr. Zuengger, who was inadequately compensated in money from the European court for nearly 15 years of legal battles over his detention.

Furthermore, the incident involving a malfunctioning street camera that incorrectly fined numerous drivers highlights systemic flaws. When the error was discovered, no refunds were issued, justified by the absurd reasoning that payment implied guilt, despite the prohibitive cost of legal action against the state.

Despite these criticisms, I acknowledge that many choose to live and work in Germany and find satisfaction here. My critique stems not from a desire to alter this reality but from the obligation to reside under a legal framework that does not resonate with my principles.

Printed in Poland
by Amazon Fulfillment
Poland Sp. z o.o., Wrocław

32325102R00054